ATVs

BY LINDSAY SHAFFER

EPIC

BELLWETHER MEDIA • MINNEAPOLIS, MN

EPIC BOOKS are no ordinary books. They burst with intense action, high-speed heroics, and shadows of the unknown. Are you ready for an Epic adventure?

This edition first published in 2019 by Bellwether Media, Inc.

No part of this publication may be reproduced in whole or in part without written permission of the publisher. For information regarding permission, write to Bellwether Media, Inc., Attention: Permissions Department, 6012 Blue Circle Drive, Minnetonka, MN 55343.

Library of Congress Cataloging-in-Publication Data

Names: Shaffer, Lindsay, author.
Title: ATVs / by Lindsay Shaffer.
Description: Minneapolis, MN : Bellwether Media, Inc., 2019. | Series: Epic.
   Full Throttle | Includes bibliographical references and index. | Audience: Ages 7-12. | Audience: Grades 2 to 7.
Identifiers: LCCN 2018002167 (print) | LCCN 2018007220 (ebook) | ISBN
   9781626178700 (hardcover : alk. paper) | ISBN 9781681036175 (ebook)
Subjects: LCSH: All terrain vehicles–Juvenile literature.
Classification: LCC TL235.6 (ebook) | LCC TL235.6 .S53 2019 (print) | DDC 629.228/8–dc23
LC record available at https://lccn.loc.gov/2018002167

Editor: Christina Leaf   Designer: Jeffrey Kollock

Printed in the United States of America, North Mankato, MN.

TABLE OF CONTENTS

TRAIL RIDING

Engines **rev** as two ATVs speed over a dirt trail. The path twists and turns tightly through tall trees. The riders punch the **throttle**. Their vehicles zoom across the rough **terrain**.

One rider soars over a jump.
The other rider races through a stream.

At the end of the trail, they slow to a stop.
They cannot wait for the next adventure!

WHAT ARE ATVs?

ATV stands for all-terrain vehicle. These vehicles are great for **off-road** driving. They can even climb boulders! Most people drive ATVs for **recreation**. Some people use them for farm or ranch work.

WORKING HARD!

Utility terrain vehicles (UTVs) can haul supplies and seat two or more people. They are great for tough jobs.

Most ATVs seat just one person. The rider **straddles** the seat while holding handlebars.

helmet

gloves

boots

Riders wear helmets, goggles, boots, and gloves. This gear helps keep them safe while they ride.

THE HISTORY OF ATVs

In 1960, a man named John Gower built the first ATV. It had six wheels. He called it the Jiger. This ATV could drive on almost any terrain. It could even drive through water!

John Gower
and the Jiger

13

ATV TIMELINE

Honda releases the first three-wheel ATV, then called ATC, or all-terrain cycle

1970

1960

The first ATV, the six-wheeled Jiger, is created in Canada

14

Suzuki starts selling the
first four-wheel ATV

1982

Three-wheel ATVs are banned
due to safety concerns

1987

In 1970, Honda released an ATV with three
wheels. In 1982, Suzuki started selling ATVs with
four wheels. Today, most people ride four-wheel
ATVs. These are also called quads or four-wheelers.

ATV PARTS

ATV riders sit on the body and steer with the handlebars. They use the throttle to control their speed. Special tires provide plenty of **traction**. A strong **suspension system** softens the shock of bumpy terrain.

suspension system

BACK TO SCHOOL

ATV owners take classes to learn riding and safety skills.

rack

ATV owners can **customize** their ATVs with special parts. Racks store extra supplies. Snowplows help with winter weather. **Winches** can tow stuck vehicles.

IDENTIFY AN ATV

throttle

handlebars

rack

engine

ATV COMPETITIONS

Most ATV **competitions** are races. Riders race on trails filled with **obstacles**.

WILD RIDE!

Hare scrambles are races through rough terrain like forests, deserts, and streams.

hill climb

Hill climbs are other popular competitions. Riders compete to go the farthest or quickest up a steep hill. All riders wear safety gear. They protect themselves while they have fun!

GLOSSARY

competitions—contests

customize—to change something to make it more personal

obstacles—objects that riders have to go around or over

off-road—on trails or dirt roads

recreation—activities done for fun

rev—to increase the speed of an engine; the engine gets louder when it revs.

straddles—sits with one leg on either side of something

suspension system—the system of springs, tires, and shocks that cushions a vehicle's ride

terrain—land

throttle—the part that controls fuel going to an engine

traction—the ability to grip a surface while moving

winches—cranks used to pull or tow objects

TO LEARN MORE

AT THE LIBRARY

Abdo, Kenny. *ATVs*. Minneapolis, Minn.: Abdo Zoom, 2018.

Maurer, Tracy Nelson. *ATV Racing*. North Mankato, Minn.: Capstone Press, 2014.

Scheff, Matt. *ATVs*. Minneapolis, Minn.: Abdo Pub., 2015.

ON THE WEB

Learning more about ATVs
is as easy as 1, 2, 3.

1. Go to www.factsurfer.com.

2. Enter "ATVs" into the search box.

3. Click the "Surf" button and you will see a list
   of related web sites.

With factsurfer.com, finding more information
is just a click away.

INDEX